CHECKERBOARD BIOGRAPHIES

KAMALA HARRIS

MEGAN BORGERT-SPANIOL

Checkerboard Library

An Imprint of Abdo Publishing

abdobooks.com

ABDOBOOKS.COM

Published by Abdo Publishing, a division of ABDO, PO Box 398166, Minneapolis, Minnesota 55439.

Printed in the United States of America, North Mankato, Minnesota
052021
092021

Design and Production: Mighty Media, Inc.
Editor: Liz Salzmann
Cover Photograph: Office of Senator Kamala Harris/Wikimedia Commons
Interior Photographs: Adam Schultz/Flickr, pp. 23, 29 (bottom); archna nautiyal/Shutterstock Images, pp. 19, 27; Gage Skidmore/Wikimedia Commons, p. 25; J. Scott Applewhite/AP Images, pp. 9, 28 (bottom); Office of Senator Kamala Harris/Wikimedia Commons, p. 11; Phil Roeder/Flickr, p. 21; rucor/Flickr, pp. 7, 28; Seth Taylor/Wikimedia Commons, p. 15; Shutterstock Images, p. 11 (paper clip); Steve Rhodes/Flickr, pp. 13, 29 (top left); United States Senate/Wikimedia Commons, p. 17; White House/Wikimedia Commons, pp. 5, 29

Library of Congress Control Number: 2021932872

Publisher's Cataloging-in-Publication Data

Names: Borgert-Spaniol, Megan, author.
Title: Kamala Harris / by Megan Borgert-Spaniol
Description: Minneapolis, Minnesota : Abdo Publishing, 2022 | Series: Checkerboard biographies | Includes online resources and index.
Identifiers: ISBN 9781532196003 (lib. bdg.) | ISBN 9781098216863 (ebook)
Subjects: LCSH: Harris, Kamala, 1964- --Juvenile literature. | Vice-Presidents--United States--Biography--Juvenile literature. | Women politicians--Biography--Juvenile literature. | African American women legislators--Biography--Juvenile literature. | Women legislators--United States--Biography--Juvenile literature.
Classification: DDC 328.73092--dc23

CONTENTS

CHAPTER 1

MAKING HISTORY

On January 20, 2021, Kamala Harris became the forty-ninth vice president of the United States. In gaining this title, Harris made history. She was the first woman and first African American to hold the office. She was also the first South Asian American to do so.

This wasn't the first time Harris made history. She had been breaking **barriers** throughout her career. In California, Harris had risen from district attorney to attorney general. Later she was elected to represent California in the US Senate. Harris's reputation as a strong leader later earned her the vice-presidential nomination.

Harris's entry into the White House marked a turning point in the United States. To many, it signaled the start of a government that represented all Americans. As Harris made history, she helped clear a path for others to follow.

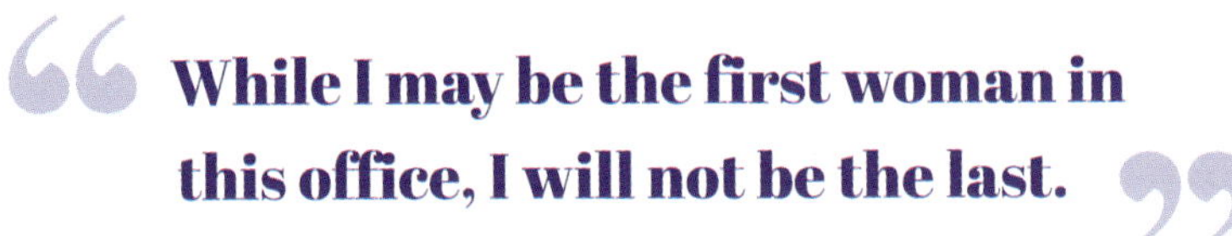

Harris was sworn in as vice president by Supreme Court Justice Sonia Sotomayor.

CHAPTER 2

LIFE LESSONS

Kamala Devi Harris was born on October 20, 1964, in Oakland, California. She had a younger sister, Maya. Kamala's parents were **immigrants**. Her mother, Shyamala, was from India. She worked as a **cancer** researcher. Kamala's father, Donald, was from Jamaica. He worked as an economics professor.

As a child, Kamala visited her father's family in Jamaica. She also visited her mother's family in India. These trips connected Kamala to the different parts of her identity.

Kamala's parents divorced in 1972. Her mother raised her and Maya. Kamala admired her mother and the example she set. Shyamala often told Kamala not to complain about a problem. Instead, she should do something about it. Kamala carried this life lesson with her into adulthood.

KAMALA IN CANADA

When Kamala was 12 years old, her mother got a job in Montreal, Québec, Canada. So, Shyamala, Kamala, and Maya moved there. Kamala lived in Montreal until she finished high school.

Kamala at five years old

CHAPTER 3

DISTRICT ATTORNEY

Harris went to college at Howard University in Washington, DC. She studied political science and economics. After graduating in 1986, she moved back to California. There, she attended the University of California's Hastings College of the Law. Harris received her law degree in 1989. The following year, she passed the **bar exam**.

In 1990, Harris became a deputy district attorney of California's Alameda County. She worked on criminal cases. Harris's job was to **prosecute** people charged with crimes.

In 2003, Harris was elected district attorney of San Francisco. She took office in 2004. Harris was the first African American woman to hold this office in California. She was also the first South Asian American woman to do so!

HOWARD UNIVERSITY

Howard University is a historically Black university. It was founded in 1867. This was a time when few US colleges admitted African Americans. Howard's mission was to primarily serve Black students.

Howard University students celebrated after Harris was elected vice president.

As district attorney, Harris started a program called Back on Track. The program was for people charged with nonviolent crimes for the first time. It gave them opportunities to better their situations. Instead of going to jail, they could work on getting an education and finding jobs.

Through efforts like Back on Track, Harris was trying to reform the criminal justice system. At the time, many other leaders spoke about being "tough on crime." Harris believed in being "smart on crime." In 2009, she published a book by this title. In it, she presents her ideas about how to reduce crime.

The same year Harris published her book, she experienced great loss. That February, her mother died of **cancer**. Shyamala's influence, however, lived on. As Harris continued her rise as a leader, she carried her mother's life lessons with her.

My parents would bring me to protests strapped tightly in my stroller, and my mother, Shyamala, raised my sister, Maya, and me to believe that it was up to us and every generation of Americans to keep on marching. ”

BIO BASICS

NAME: Kamala Devi Harris

NICKNAME: called "Momala" by her stepchildren

BIRTH: October 20, 1964, Oakland, California

SPOUSE: Doug Emhoff (2014-present)

STEPCHILDREN: Cole and Ella

FAMOUS FOR: becoming the first woman, first African American, and first South Asian American to be vice president of the United States

ACHIEVEMENTS: being elected district attorney of San Francisco and attorney general of California; being elected to represent California in the US Senate; being elected vice president of the United States

CHAPTER 4

ATTORNEY GENERAL

In 2010, Harris was ready for a new chapter in her career. She ran for attorney general of California. In this job, she would oversee California's Department of Justice. The election was close, but Harris won. She beat **Republican** Steve Cooley by less than 1 percent of the vote.

Harris was **inaugurated** on January 3, 2011. She was the first woman, first South Asian American, and first African American to serve as California's attorney general. As attorney general, Harris continued her efforts to be "smart on crime." She also focused on education and protecting citizens from financial **scams**.

In addition to her career accomplishments, Harris also celebrated big events in her personal life. In 2014, she married lawyer Doug Emhoff. This made her stepmother to Emhoff's two children, Cole and Ella.

In 2015, Harris launched OpenJustice. This website shared criminal justice data with the public. OpenJustice included data on arrests, use of force by police officers, and more. The website's goal was to improve public

Harris received the nomination for California attorney general on June 8, 2010.

safety. It was also to expose and address **racism** and other problems in the criminal justice system.

In January 2015, California Senator Barbara Boxer had announced that she would retire. Harris decided to run for Boxer's open seat. She was ready for a new challenge.

In her campaign for senator, Harris told Californians what she would do if elected. She said she would continue to fight for criminal justice reform. Harris also wanted to increase the **minimum wage**.

Harris ran against fellow **Democrat** Loretta Sanchez. In November 2016, Harris won the election by more than 20 percent of the vote. She would be the first African American to represent California in the US Senate.

In her acceptance speech, Harris said, "Part of what makes us great is fighting for our ideals. And this is the moment that is challenging us. I know we will rise to the occasion." Harris was a rising leader, and her next stop was the US Senate!

Do not despair. Do not be overwhelmed. Do not throw up our hands when it is time to roll up our sleeves and fight for who we are. ”

In 2014, Harris gave a speech at a celebration of the fiftieth anniversary of the Civil Rights Act of 1964.

CHAPTER 5

SENATOR HARRIS

Harris was sworn into the US Senate in January 2017. This made her the first South Asian American senator. And, she was only the second African American woman senator.

Harris served on several Senate committees. One was the US Senate Select Committee on Intelligence. On this committee, Harris and the other members dealt with national security. This included investigating Russian influence in the 2016 US presidential election.

Harris also served on the Judiciary Committee. She and the other members considered people nominated to the US **Supreme Court**. These included Neil Gorsuch and Brett Kavanaugh. Harris became known for asking smart, tough questions during their confirmation hearings.

As a senator, Harris also worked to create new laws. She supported **environmental** protections. This included laws that banned offshore drilling in certain areas. Harris

I see part of my responsibility on the [Intelligence] Committee as helping make sure no one is above the law.

Harris was sworn in as senator by Vice President Joe Biden (*right*).

worked to defend the rights of **immigrants** and the **LGBT** community. She also fought for affordable health care for all Americans.

In January 2019, Harris published a book called *The Truths We Hold: An American Journey*. The book gave readers an inside look at Harris's upbringing, education, and career. Harris was now more widely known than ever before. And she was ready to climb to a new level of leadership.

The same month her book came out, Harris made an exciting announcement. A presidential election would be taking place the following year. Harris would be running for the **Democratic** nomination!

EVERYDAY HEROES

Harris wrote a children's book called *Superheroes Are Everywhere*. It is about regular people helping to make the world a better place. The book was published in 2019.

I'm honored to be considered a 'first,' but I always think about the people who came before and paved the way for me to get where I am today.

Harris at the San Francisco Pride Parade in 2019

CHAPTER 6

RUNNING FOR PRESIDENT

Harris was one of more than twenty Democrats campaigning for president. Many of them were experienced leaders like Harris. Some, including Senator Bernie Sanders and former vice president Joe Biden, had many loyal supporters. But Harris managed to stand out among the crowd of contenders.

In a June 2019 **debate**, Harris criticized the policies of the nation's **Republican** president. But she also challenged Biden, one of her Democratic opponents. She criticized Biden's voting record from when he was a US senator. Harris's performance at the debate drew attention. After that night, many considered her to be a strong candidate.

Harris had the support of many Americans. But by the fall of 2019, her campaign was struggling financially. Some Democrats started dropping out of the race for president. In December 2019, Harris dropped out

Harris visited a kindergarten class in Des Moines, Iowa, during her presidential campaign.

too. She told her supporters it was one of the hardest decisions of her life. Harris returned to the Senate.

The year 2020 was difficult for the United States. That May, in Minneapolis, Minnesota, a man named George Floyd died while being arrested by the police. People across the nation protested Floyd's death. Americans demanded that local and national leaders address **racism** in law enforcement.

Harris was one of the leaders who took action. After Floyd's death, she attended peaceful protests in Washington, DC. She called for policies that would help end racial **discrimination** in policing.

Meanwhile, the campaigns for the **Democratic** presidential nomination continued. By August 2020, it was clear that Joe Biden would be the nominee. He would soon choose a running mate. Many Americans believed Harris would make a good vice president. Biden agreed. On August 11, he announced Harris as his running mate!

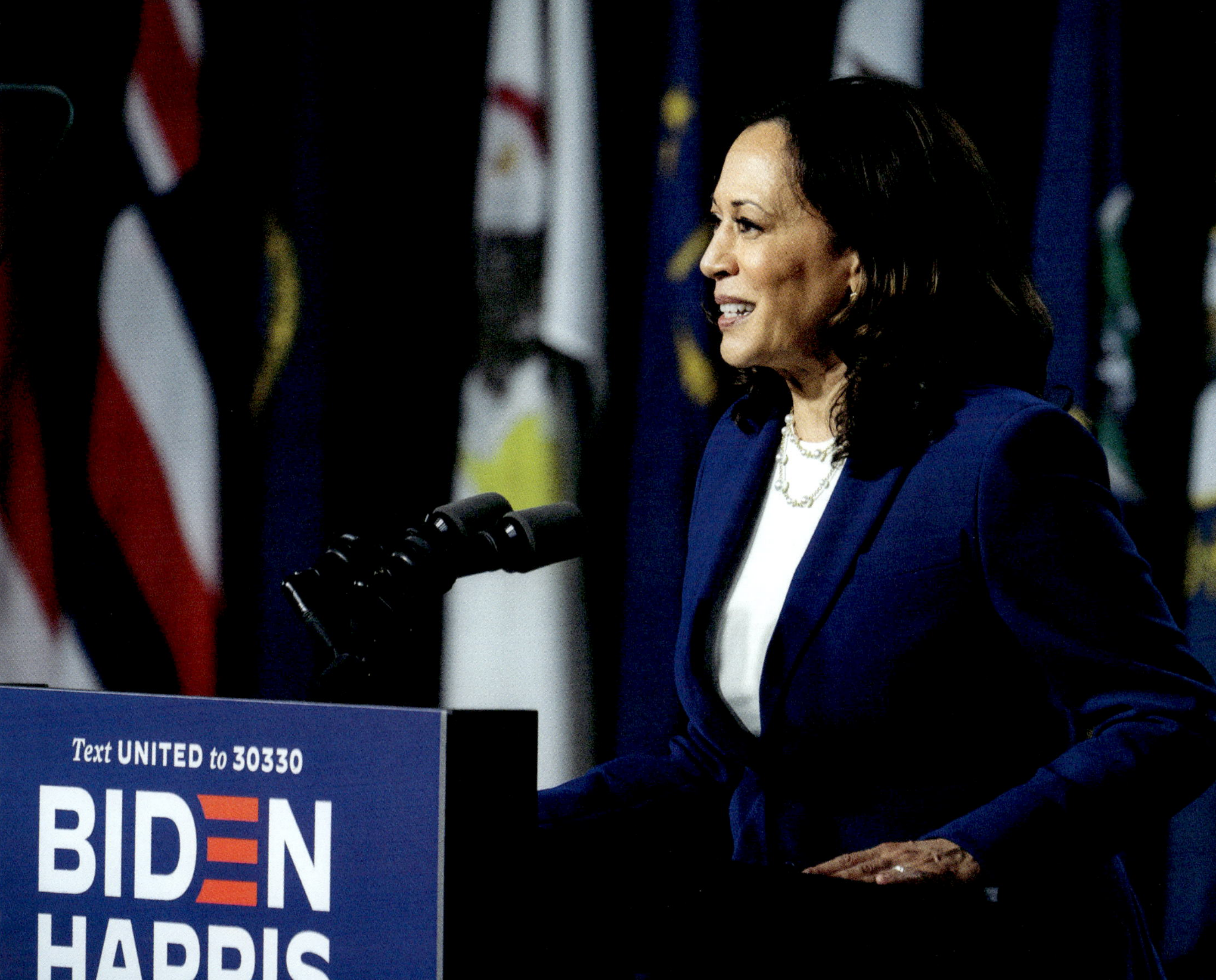

Harris speaks to voters after becoming the vice-presidential candidate.

CHAPTER 7

VP-ELECT

Once again, Harris had her sights set on the White House. This time, she was teaming up with a former opponent. Harris and Biden had argued during **debates** the previous year. But they agreed with each other on many issues. They campaigned for affordable health care, protecting the **environment**, and improving racial equality.

Harris and Biden also had a plan for how to address another crisis. As the election approached, the United States was in the grip of the **COVID-19 pandemic**. By October 2020, more than 200,000 Americans had died from the disease. Biden and Harris presented their ideas for fighting the pandemic. Their plan included safety measures, increased testing, and more.

On November 3, millions of Americans cast their votes for the next president. More people voted in the 2020 election than in any previous election! The winner would be either Biden or the current **Republican** president, Donald Trump. Often, winners can be declared within a day or so of the election. But 2020 was different.

Actors Nnamdi Asomugha (*left*) and Kerry Washington campaigned for Biden and Harris in 2020. They wore face masks to protect themselves from COVID-19.

Because of the **pandemic**, many Americans mailed in their votes. They did so to avoid spreading **COVID-19** at crowded voting locations. The large number of mail-in votes made it take longer to count them all. Finally, on November 7, the winners were declared. Biden would be the next US president. And Harris would be the next vice president!

CHAPTER 8

MADAM VICE PRESIDENT

The presidential inauguration took place on January 20, 2021. During the ceremony, Harris was sworn in as vice president. This was a historic moment. Harris was the first woman to be vice president of the United States. She was also the first African American and first South Asian American to hold the office.

After the inauguration, Harris got to work. She swore in new senators and members of Biden's **cabinet**. She took calls with other world leaders. And she sat in meetings with Biden regarding handling the **COVID-19 pandemic**.

As Harris worked, the nation watched. Harris had broken through many **barriers** on her way to the White House. Many Americans expected her to do great things as Madam Vice President!

Dream with ambition, lead with conviction, and see yourselves in a way that others may not, simply because they've never seen it before.

Throughout her career, Harris has been guided by the words, "Kamala Harris, for the people."

TIMELINE

1964

Kamala Devi Harris is born on October 20 in Oakland, California.

1986

Harris graduates from Howard University.

1989

Harris receives her law degree from the University of California's Hastings College of the Law.

1990

Harris begins her career as a deputy district attorney of California's Alameda County.

2004

Harris becomes the district attorney of San Francisco.

2011

Harris becomes the attorney general of California.

2019

In January, Harris announces her campaign to be the Democratic presidential candidate. She drops out of the race in December.

2021

In January, Harris takes office as Vice President of the United States.

2016

Harris is elected to represent California in the US Senate.

2020

Democratic presidential candidate Joe Biden chooses Harris as his running mate in August. Harris and Biden win the election in November.

GLOSSARY

bar exam—a test a person must pass in order to become a lawyer.

barrier—something that blocks the way or makes something difficult.

cabinet—a group of advisers chosen by the president to lead government departments.

cancer—any of a group of often deadly diseases marked by harmful changes in the normal growth of cells. Cancer can spread and destroy healthy tissues and organs.

COVID-19—a serious illness that first appeared in late 2019.

debate—a public discussion about a question or topic.

Democrat—a member of the Democratic political party. Democrats believe in social change and strong government.

discrimination (dihs-krih-muh-NAY-shuhn)—unfair treatment, often based on race, religion, or gender.

environment—nature and everything in it, such as the land, sea, and air.

immigrant—a person who enters another country to live.

inaugurate (ih-NAW-gyuh-rayt)—to swear into a political office. The ceremony in which a person is inaugurated is an inauguration.

LGBT—stands for lesbian, gay, bisexual, transgender.

minimum wage—the lowest hourly wage a company is allowed to pay its workers.

pandemic—an outbreak of a disease that spreads quickly throughout the world.

prosecute—to bring before a court of law.

racism—the belief that one race is better than another.

Republican—a member of the Republican political party. Republicans are conservative and believe in small government.

scam—a fake or illegal act or operation.

Supreme Court—the highest, most powerful court in the United States.

ONLINE RESOURCES

To learn more about Kamala Harris, please visit **abdobooklinks.com** or scan this QR code. These links are routinely monitored and updated to provide the most current information available.

INDEX